HOW TO BEAT THE CREDIT BUREAUS

The Insider's Guide to Consumer Credit

BOB HAMMOND

PALADIN PRESS
BOULDER, COLORADO

Also by Bob Hammond:

The Credit Repair Rip-off:
  How to Avoid the Scams and Do It Yourself
Credit Secrets: How to Erase Bad Credit
Life after Debt: The Complete Credit
  Restoration Kit

to Damaris

How to Beat the Credit Bureaus:
The Insider's Guide to Consumer Credit
by Bob Hammond
Copyright © 1990 by Bob Hammond

ISBN 0-87364-557-X
Printed in the United States of America

Published by Paladin Press, a division of
Paladin Enterprises, Inc., P.O. Box 1307,
Boulder, Colorado 80306, USA.
(303) 443-7250

Direct inquires and/or orders to the above address.

CONTENTS

FOREWORD

Upon learning that this book was going to be published, I was reminded of a young congressman who was elected to high office recently. Very anxiously, the lawmaker approached the whip and asked, "Do you think I should take part in the debate today?" The wise man thought for a moment and then answered, "I think you should remain silent. It would be better for people to wonder why you didn't speak than to wonder why you did."

The same advice could have been—and more than likely was—given to Bob Hammond in tackling an area as volatile and controversial as the relationship between big business and consumer credit. But I know Bob to be a man of mature intellect and immense courage. I applaud his decision to march to the beat of a different drummer as he leads readers through the "four Es" of credit consulting: Erase, Establish, Educate, Encourage. His book is must reading for every educator and parent in America today.

Ken Yarbrough, Executive Director
Consumer Credit Commission

ACKNOWLEDGMENTS

I want to thank Lenny Robin, chief executive officer of Fresh Start Financial Services, for providing me with much essential information regarding a complicated and sometimes frightening subject.

I'm also grateful to everyone at Paladin Press for their willingness to publish controversial ideas and for their professional assistance to me as a writer.

A special thanks also goes out to Tom Hall for encouraging me to strive for excellence.

And finally, thanks to Darlene Taylor for the hours she spent deciphering my handwriting.

"Invisible changes are taking place in the credit card industry, and they are cataclysmic. There is an abysmal ignorance on the subject because the stakes are high (to the people who control the system) in terms of ignoring the whole question. This is leading to a significant kind of tyranny. The key democratic principle of a man's control over his life is being abused. And unless we do something, we're suddenly going to wake up and realize we're a nation of slaves."

—Ralph Nader

INTRODUCTION

Every day an organized gang of perpetrators commits a crime against millions of innocent citizens. Caught in the grasp of a powerful syndicate, countless individuals are violated, humiliated, and defiled. Their feeble protests are met with mockery as they are mercilessly victimized. Those who would dare fight back are silenced.

The purpose of this book is to alert you to a clear and present danger within our society that thrives upon human frailty and imperfection. It is a dehumanizing rape of justice, and it has gone unchallenged for too long. The victims are innocent consumers trapped within a deceptive web of information

1

systems. The perpetrators are members of powerful corporations known as consumer reporting agencies, or credit bureaus.

What you are about to read may disturb you, frighten you, or cause you to be outraged. That is not my intention, however. Rather, it is my sincere hope that by reading this book you will become awakened to your power as an individual. It is my conviction that by studying and applying the ideas herein, you will discover your ability to fight back against an unfair system and win. By coming to understand the nature of the beast, you will become empowered to overcome it.

We will begin by taking an inside look at the major credit bureaus. You will discover how information about your habits and lifestyle is secretly gathered, processed, and published in the form of credit reports. You will find out how the various agencies freely exchange information about you and how your file is identified and categorized. Most importantly, you will learn how to obtain copies of this information, how to interpret what they say about you, and how to fight back.

PART ONE

INSIDE THE MAJOR CREDIT BUREAUS

If you're like most adult American consumers, you probably have at least one item of inaccurate, misleading, or obsolete information in your credit bureau files. In many cases, you will find information about someone else with a similar name. In other cases, accounts that were paid promptly and satisfactorily will be reported as late payments or bad debts.

Regardless of its inaccuracy, such information can cause you to be turned down for credit cards, loans, mortgages, insurance, or even employment. You, the consumer, are forced to pay the price of rejection, humiliation, and usurious interest rates because of someone else's mistakes. Meanwhile, these bureaucratic Goliaths continue to operate above the law, free to indict innocent citizens for crimes they didn't commit (or, just as bad, to brand someone a second-class citizen for a mistake that was made as many as ten years ago).

According to these corporate pharisees, you are guilty until proven innocent. Those who would come to your assistance are accused of being liars and thieves. Why else do you think there has been such a tirade of negative publicity aimed at the so-called "credit-clinics"? Why have a number of independent credit bureaus been shut down as soon as they opened?

Of those who have attempted to speak out, many have been ridiculed or silenced. Others have sold out to the system. But there will always remain a few who refuse to "bow their knee to Baal." They are the ones who loudly proclaim, "I'm mad as hell and I'm not going to take it anymore!" With courage, they will take hold of the sword of truth and slay the dragon of deceit. Only then shall the rest of us regain that which has been lost—our birthright of freedom and dignity.

CHAPTER ONE

BIG BROTHER IS WATCHING YOU

In George Orwell's classic novel, *1984*, Big Brother was portrayed as an all-seeing, all-knowing overlord. He was exalted as the great ruler of society to whom all honor and obedience was due—without question. In every home, a television screen served not only as an instrument of propaganda, but as a twenty-four-hour monitor of the inhabitants' every move. There was no escaping the all-seeing eye of Big Brother.

In fact, *1984* was somewhat prophetic. Perhaps it is coincidental, but in the year 1984, TRW, one of the largest credit reporting agencies in the world, successfully lobbied for legislation that severely restricted your ability to question the authority of the credit bureaus. This law, known as the Credit Services Act, will be described in detail in a later chapter.

First, let's take a look inside the major credit bureaus, where Big Brother's internal mechanisms actually operate.

CHAPTER TWO

INFORMATION GATHERING

The moment an individual consumer applies for credit, the process of credit reporting begins and the bureau's monitoring process is initiated. The information supplied in a person's credit application is used to find or establish a file at one or more credit bureaus. This is known as the inquiry process.

Lending institutions subscribe to credit bureaus in order to obtain the credit and payment history of potential applicants. In turn, many of these subscribers report the payment patterns and credit histories of their own borrowers to the bureaus. Besides creditors and other financial institutions such as banks, retailers, mortgage lenders, and oil companies, a bureau's subscribers may include other credit bureaus, insurance companies, collection agencies, employers and professional organizations such as medical and dental groups. In addition, credit bureaus supply information to government agencies such as the IRS, FBI, welfare departments, and local police.

Credit bureaus also obtain information from public records. This information may include bankruptcy filings, arrests, judgments, tax liens, wage garnishments, notices of default, and so on. Generally, this process of information gathering is done by poorly paid clerical employees. Not surprisingly, this often leads to a number of incorrect entries on the consumer's credit report.

One of the bureaus' functions is to blindly enter any information provided to them by their subscribers. There are many instances where the bureau may report inaccurate, erroneous, incomplete, obsolete, and misleading information without ever being aware of doing so. Sometimes they are aware that the information is incorrect but refuse to update or delete it. This is what we will later refer to as "willful noncompliance."

Members of the Associated Credit Bureaus, Inc., a large trade organization, may also subscribe to a service that provides information on individuals' credit accounts with large national and regional creditors. Then, whenever the need arises, a bureau can obtain a complete report on an individual from another bureau. This service is often used when a person who is new to a community applies for credit. In such cases, the local bureau has no credit file on the individual, and so has to request a report from the bureau in the area where the person used to live.

Associated Credit Bureaus, Inc. represents most

of the nation's major credit bureaus. This powerful organization symbolizes the colossal growth of the credit information industry, with over two thousand member bureaus employing more than thirty thousand persons. Each year, these credit bureaus supply approximately four hundred thousand subscribers with more than fifty million brief "factual" summaries.

Although most credit bureaus are small local monopolies serving communities of twenty thousand or fewer households, computerization has allowed a few to operate virtually nationwide. The following is a list of the five largest credit bureaus in the United States. Together they maintain more than 150 million individual credit records.

TRW Credit Information Services
505 City Parkway West
Orange, CA 92667
(714) 991-5100

Trans Union Credit Information
444 North Michigan Ave.
Chicago, IL 60611
(312) 645-6000

CBI/Equifax (formerly Retail Credit Co.)
P.O. Box 4091
Atlanta, GA 30302
(404) 329-1725

Associated Credit Services, Inc. (formerly Pinger System)
624 E. North Belt, Suite 400
Houston, TX 77060
(713) 878-1900

Chilton Credimatic Corporation
12606 Greenville Ave.
Dallas, TX 75243
(214) 699-6111

Your local credit bureaus can be located through the Yellow Pages under Credit Bureaus or Credit Reporting Agencies. Or you may contact the trade organization:

Associated Credit Bureaus, Inc.
16211 Park Place 10
P.O. Box 218300
Houston, TX 77218
(713) 492-8155

In April 1988, TRW acquired Chilton Corporation. As of this writing, the two companies were still in the process of merging information into a common data base. On January 30, 1989, Associated Credit Services (formerly Pinger System), of Houston, Texas, began merging its data base with that of CBI/Equifax.

At this rate, we will soon see the elimination of the small independent bureaus as three monolithic giants emerge. TRW, Trans Union, and CBI/Equifax will then reign as the unchallenged rulers of society.

CHAPTER THREE

INVESTIGATIVE REPORTS

In addition to credit reports, consumer reporting agencies maintain files on individuals containing other subjective information obtained through interviews and inquiries of neighbors, business associates, employers, and other record-keeping institutions. The "stated" purpose of such information is to "protect" clients from individuals who falsify—or fail to reveal—significant information that could affect credit, insurance, or employment decisions.

Insurance companies are prime examples of clients who rely upon such investigative reports to help make their decisions. In such cases, negative information is the bureaus' most saleable product. Clients pay to find out whether there is any information which warrants classifying the applicant as a bad risk—and therefore a possible monetary loss to the company.

Investigative reports are compiled by field workers rather than computers. The bureaus stress high productivity and low operating costs in order to meet demand. They also save time and money by relying on previously reported information in their own in-house files. This often results in adverse information being reported repeatedly—regardless of its accuracy. This can mean recurring problems for an individual over a period of years.

Consider the example of CBI/Equifax. This Atlanta-based company maintains files on more than 40 million individuals throughout the United States. The company employs approximately 5,200 investigators, or field representatives, who talk to about 150,000 people a day. That averages about thirty daily conversations per investigator (if the company's statistics are to be believed).

In 1974, when CBI/Equifax was still known as Retail Credit Company, four of the firm's investigators testified before Wisconsin Senator William Proxmire's Subcommittee on Consumer Credit. All four employees testified that the company required them to produce adverse information on 6 to 10 percent of insurance applicants. The basic philosophy of the credit bureaus was this: a massive amount of derogatory information proves that a reporting agency is being more thorough and professional than its competitors. More adverse information resulted in obtaining more contracts.

In one incident, a woman was denied car insurance because her investigative report included a neighbor's comment identifying her as "a lady of the evening." A subsequent check with ten other neighbors showed that the information was false. The report was based on a single interview with the "neighborhood crackpot." According to testimony, many similar reports were fabricated as a "time-saving device."

The following are some of the typical questions asked by credit bureau employees in compiling investigative consumer reports.

- Any criticism of neighborhood?
- Premises poorly kept?
- Personal/family reputation or associates questionable?
- Any criminal record?
- Illegal or unfair business practices or dealings?
- Heavy debts?
- Domestic troubles?
- Arrests?
- Reckless driving?
- Any use of marijuana, LSD, heroin, or other drugs?
- Any criticism of character or associates?
- Is general reputation as to reliability, habits, and morality at all questionable?

Anyone who has ever applied for credit, insurance, or even a job is subject to having an investigative report compiled. In many cases, individuals have been rejected, humiliated, and treated like second-class citizens based solely upon erroneous information. In some cases, the report is even compiled on the wrong person. This brings us to our next subject.

CHAPTER FOUR

IDENTIFICATION SYSTEMS

Have you ever wondered how the bureaus are able to tell the difference between all of the people with similar names? How many John Smiths do you suppose there are in the United States?

The identification system is the "weak link" of the credit bureaus. Each bureau has its own system of sequential patterns that are designed to protect the security of each individual file. The intent is to identify each file in such a manner as to separate individuals with similar names so that the contents of the file of John B. Smith from Kansas City will not appear on the file of John B. Smith from Atlanta. But what if there are two John

B. Smiths in Kansas City?

As you may have guessed, your Social Security number has come to play an important part in identifying you as an individual. But what if someone else happens to "make up" a Social Security number that coincides with yours? Or, what if the clerk who enters your credit application into the system accidently transposes a number? Will that automatically merge your report with someone else's? Or will it cause a new credit file to be created?

So far, no bureau has come up with a perfect file identification system. That is why you will often see items on your report that belong to someone else with a similar name. In an effort to maintain maximum efficiency, the credit bureaus would rather set up more than one file on a single person than to risk merging several people's files into one. This is the "Achilles' heel" that has allowed a number of individuals to circumvent the system.

Some people have tried to bypass the system by deliberately changing their Social Security numbers or dates of birth. These methods are generally ineffective and often result in the addition of a "Checkpoint," "TRANS-ALERT," or other potential fraud indicator to the file. Others have tried "borrowing" the credit of someone with a similar name. An article in *Newsweek* (September 12, 1988) reported that certain unethical credit repair clinics were selling the credit histories of people with good credit to people with bad credit. This highly illegal practice resulted in the arrest of dozens of credit thieves and greedy consumers.

The only legitimate way to "start over" is to create a brand new credit file. First, however, it is necessary to understand the identification systems used by each of the major bureaus. Only then is it possible to circumvent the identification systems of each bureau and "start over" with a file that says, "NO RECORD FOUND."

Also known as "file segregation," this unique method of starting over has been used by individuals from all walks of life. This technique is so effective in erasing a bad credit record—literally overnight—that certain consultants are charging fees of up to three thousand dollars to set up new credit files for their clients. According to a leading bankruptcy attorney, "The file segregation method is perhaps the only 100 percent successful method of credit repair."

A complete description of the file segregation method, including the identification systems used by all of the major credit bureaus in the United States, is included in my previous book, *Credit Secrets: How to Erase Bad Credit*, published by Paladin Press.

HOW TO READ YOUR CREDIT REPORT

When reading or analyzing a credit report, it is important to know what to expect and what should be on the report. All credit bureaus have a number of points in common. Each bureau, however, has its own particular format and special codes. This is intended to foster your dependence upon them as authorities.

The first section of the report is composed of the information used to identify you, the subject of the report. This section will consist of your complete name, your current address (or the address you listed on the application), previous address (especially if you've been less than two years at your present one), your Social Security number, and your date of birth. This section may also include your spouse's name, your place of employment, your previous place of employment, your occupation, and your telephone number.

The next section consists of your credit history. This part of the report consists of such information as the names and dates of any accounts opened, the credit limits of each account, the terms originally issued, the outstanding balances, your monthly payment schedule, and how you have adhered to that schedule. Your performance is rated as to promptness (one-, two-, or three-month late indicators). Accounts are usually listed as R (revolving) or I (installment), with a rating of 1 through 9 to indicate the status of the account. A 1 represents current or paid, 2 indicates late payments, and so on up to 9, which indicates that the account was written off as a bad debt. This section will also include items pertaining to your accounts, such as cosigners/signers, joint accounts, and collateral.

The next section of your report is a listing of inquiries. Every time you apply for credit, an inquiry is made into your credit file and will be listed in your report. The name of the inquiring company (the subscriber) will be listed along with a subscriber number and date of inquiry.

In many cases, individuals have been denied credit because of excessive inquiries on their report. Although not considered a negative remark in itself, an inquiry gives the creditor the impression that you have been turned down elsewhere. Too many inquiries make the individual appear desperate and thus a poor credit risk. The states regulate the amount of time inquiries may remain on your report; in many cases it is as long as twenty-four months.

One of the problems with the inquiry process is that many times a consumer will end up with inquiries which were never authorized. This is often the case when an individual looks to purchase a new or used car. In "shopping the loan," the finance manager will often fax the credit application to several banks and finance companies at the same time. Each institution will then order a separate credit report, thus generating a series of inquiries on the unsuspecting consumer's report. If the individual decides not to purchase the car—for any reason—he is still left with the job of explaining the numerous inquiries to subsequent potential credit grantors.

The August 1989 edition of *Commission Update* (the monthly newsletter of the Consumer Credit Commission) revealed that Chevron Oil Company has made a practice of making several back-to-back inquiries on each applicant for its credit card, thus causing that individual to be declined credit from competing credit card companies.

The next section of your report will list public record information. It may contain a history of bankruptcy filings, judgments, arrests, tax liens, and foreclosures. If you have defaulted on a government loan or have had a wage garnishment, that information will be listed in this section.

The final section of a credit report is one not often found and one about which most people are unaware. This section is known as the Consumer Statement, or Statement of Dispute. This is where you, the consumer, may file your own side of the story if you disagree with any of the information reported. You have the right to include any statement—up to one hundred words in length—about anything you wish to clarify on your credit report. More about this in the section entitled, *Fighting Back.*

CHAPTER SIX

FRAUD INDICATORS

In recent years, TRW developed a fraud detection system known as Checkpoint. It was originally designed to point an accusing finger at the individual who was attempting to create a new credit file by changing his name or Social Security number. Today, practically every credit report has a Checkpoint.

Credit grantors have been educated to assume that every Checkpoint is an indicator of potential fraud. In most cases, however, it is simply a case of a clerical error on the part of the clerk or salesperson. When the information from the credit application is transferred to the computer terminal, a number or letter is often transposed or entered incorrectly. This results in a Checkpoint on your TRW report.

According to published literature, a Checkpoint appears as follows:

((((CHECKPOINT))) SS# NOT ISSUED AS OF 6/89

This checkpoint message appears on the TRW report if the applicant's Social Security number has not been issued as of the date displayed in the message.

((((CHECKPOINT))) SS# IS 555123456

This checkpoint message appears when the information in TRW's file relating to the applicant's Social Security number, generation (Jr., Sr., III, etc.), or year of birth does not correspond to the information entered in the subscriber's inquiry. It is possible that the information was entered incorrectly or does not even pertain to the individual.

((((CHECKPOINT))) AKA PRESENT ON
FILE. MORE DATA MAY BE
AVAILABLE UNDER AKA.

When this message appears on the TRW report, it indicates that there may be additional information under the name following the message:

ATTN FILE VARIATION: 1ST NAME IS JON

A file variation message will appear whenever a difference exists between the inquiry information and the name and address information listed on file. Again, it is possible that the information may not pertain to the individual.

— FILE IDENT: MID INIT IS J

A file ident message will appear when information is not given on input but exists in the file.

CAUTION THE ABOVE REPORT MAY
CONTAIN ITEMS FOR OTHER MEMBERS
OF THE SAME FAMILY.

This message may appear when names and addresses are similar. It means that closer checking of the applicant or with the application may be necessary. This message is very common in cases of Jr. and Sr.

FACS (Fraud Application Control Seminar) is another security watch program used by TRW. Recent consumer complaints indicate that FACS may display messages on a credit report which have adverse connotations. One such message indicated that the consumer was somehow associated with a credit consultant who coincidentally had an office suite in the same building as the consumer. The consumer in this case was a licensed physician who, although qualified for credit in every respect, was denied because of the erroneous message. FACS also indicates addresses which have been identified as mail forwarding services.

Trans Union uses a fraud prevention system known as TRANS-ALERT, which highlights potential discrepancies between the information applicants provide and Trans Union's file information. The following are examples of TRANS-ALERT messages which may appear on your credit report from Trans Union.

TRANS-ALERT: INPUT ADDRESS DOES NOT MATCH FILE ADDRESS

This message alerts the subscriber to several possibilities about the subject's file. Perhaps the person has just moved, so the new address can be investigated. Maybe the address was input incorrectly from the application. Or (what the subscriber is really thinking), the applicant could be using another person's file in order to gain credit approval.

TRANS-ALERT: INPUT SSN NOT ISSUED

If the input Social Security number does not match Trans Union's table of government-provided, valid SSNs, the above message will be displayed.

This indicates to the subscriber that you could be falsifying a Social Security number in an attempt to create a new credit file.

***TRANS-ALERT: 4 INQUIRIES IN
LAST 60 DAYS***

Multiple inquiries made on a single subject within in a short period of time are used to signal the credit grantor that increased attention may be needed.

Trans Union also introduced HAWK—"The Credit Fraud Predator"—in 1988. This in-house system augments the automatic Trans-Alert messages.

The HAWK system automatically retrieves relevant data from the input information. It then matches this data against Trans Union's table of suspect information. When HAWK finds a match or several matches, it produces "HAWK-ALERT" messages in the Trans Union credit report to highlight potential fraud. For example, ***HAWK-ALERT: VERIFY INPUT ADDRESS/TELEPHONE NUMBER*** will appear before the "END OF CREDIT REPORT" message. Depending on the situation, HAWK might display nine other messages.

Trans Union obtains HAWK file information from several sources, including:

- Yellow Page directory listings of check-cashing offices, mail drops, and telephone-answering services
- Government agencies
- Addresses, Social Security numbers, and telephone numbers from applications

HAWK's file also contains credit bureaus' internal files providing addresses verified as being vacant lots, and SSNs of deceased persons.

CBI/Equifax has a similar program called DTEC. With no clue other than a Social Security number, DTEC can track down the current addresses of individuals whose addresses are no longer—or never have been—valid, or who have given inaccurate or incomplete names. DTEC also alerts the subscriber to potential fraud by displaying such messages as:

- Social Security number out of range
- Social Security number reported retired
- Social Security number misused

All of the major credit bureaus incorporate security watch programs. Listed below are the names of some of the more widely used programs.

- **TRW**—Checkpoint, AKA NIXIE, Decode, FACS (Fraud Application Control Seminar), SAFE (Security Awareness and Fraud Education), FOF (Focus on Fraud).
- **TRANS UNION**—TRANS-ALERT, HAWK, TRACE, DELPHI, UNISSN (Uniting Social Security Numbers with the complete credit files of people under their various names and addresses.)
- **CBI/Equifax**—LINK II, DTEC, SAFESCAN, Snowball, Delinquency Alert System, SWITCH.
- **Chilton**—Auto Alert, Security Watch
- **Associated**—SENTRY

CHAPTER SEVEN

HOW THE BUREAUS RAPE YOUR CREDIT

The bureaus use five distinct methods to gather negative information. These include computerized nine-track tape (used by credit grantors to record payment and balance information on customers and then transferred to the bureaus by computer), manual forms, instant updates, inquiries, and public records. Positive information is generally obtained by only one method: computerized nine-track tape. The Fair Credit Reporting Act deals specifically with the reporting of negative information; it does not cover the reporting of positive information.

The information on your credit report is generally categorized by three ratings: POSITIVE, NEUTRAL, and NEGATIVE. The following are the only statements on your credit report that are considered POSITIVE:

1. Paid satisfactorily (no late payments)
2. Current account (with no late payments)

The following are considered NEUTRAL (In reality, anything less than a POSITIVE rating is considered NEGATIVE):

1. Paid
2. Settled
3. Refinanced
4. Inquiry
5. Credit card lost/stolen
6. Current (was 30 days late)
7. Paid (was 30 days late)

The following are considered NEGATIVE:

1. Bankruptcies—Chapter 7 or 13
2. Judgment
3. Tax lien
4. Account closed—grantor's request
5. Paid (was 60, 90 or 120 days late)
6. SCNL—subscriber cannot locate
7. Paid (collection)
8. Paid (charge-off)
9. BK liq. reo. (bankruptcy liquidation reorganization)
10. Charge-off
11. Collection account
12. Delinquent
13. Current (was 60, 90 or 120 days late)
14. Checkpoint, TRANS-ALERT, or Caution (potential fraud indicators)
15. Excessive inquiries

As you can see, the deck is stacked against you. It's a lot easier to accumulate negative information in your files than it is to obtain positive data. Once again, the philosophy of the credit bureau is that a massive amount of derogatory information proves that a reporting agency is being more thorough and professional than its competitors. In other words, negative data sells reports!

Although there is no statute of limitations for the reporting of positive information, the credit bureaus like to have it removed from your file within five years. Negative information, on the other hand, may be reported for up to seven years. Bankruptcy may be reported for as long as ten years. Notice that I used the words "may be reported." In other words, The bureaus are not *required* to report the negative information for that duration; they simply *prefer* to do so in order to add to the marketability of their reports. This, in essence, is how the bureaus rape your credit.

A CASE IN POINT

On December 5, 1988, Los Angeles Channel 2 (CBS) News Commentator Judd MacElvane revealed a story that confirmed what many people had already come to realize. The letters TRW (in this case) could have stood for "The Report's Wrong." Judd was able to get special attention at TRW on one case where negative credit information appeared on the wrong file. A consumer was attempting to buy a home but was denied credit because of a negative report from TRW. The negative information on the credit report did not even belong to the individual. The consumer attempted to resolve the matter himself but felt helpless, so he called the Action Line of Channel 2 (1-800-TV2-JUDD). Judd contacted TRW's public affairs department. Instead of the usual runaround, TRW agreed to correct the mistake and notify the lending institution of the error immediately.

Of course, had the consumer not been assisted by a professional consumer advocate armed with the persuasive force of the media, he would have had a much more difficult time getting TRW to cooperate. In many similar cases, the bureaus have either ignored such requests or simply refused to investigate the matter. In other instances, they have been so slow in responding that the consumer has suffered severe financial hardship as a result.

CHAPTER EIGHT

QUESTIONS AND ANSWERS

Q: What is a consumer reporting agency?

A: A consumer reporting agency is a company commonly called a credit bureau. A credit bureau is a business organization that puts together a report about your past credit performance, keeps the information up-to-date, and furnishes the information for a fee, in the form of credit reports to merchants, credit card issuers, insurance companies, and potential employers.

Q: Do I have the right to know what is in my credit file?

A: The Fair Credit Reporting Act gives all consumers the right to know what is in their credit files at credit bureaus.

Q: What kind of information is contained in my credit file?

A: Your credit file contains several different types of information:

1. Identifying information, such as name, address, and Social Security number.
2. Information concerning your current employment, such as the position you hold, length of employment, and income.
3. Information about your personal history, such as date of birth, number of dependents, previous addresses, and information about previous employment.
4. Information about your credit history, such as how promptly you made payments to previous creditors.
5. Information about you that is available publicly, such as records of arrests, indictments, convictions, lawsuits, tax liens, marriages, bankruptcies and court judgments.

Q: Who may obtain a copy of my credit file?

A: Only someone with a legitimate business need may see your credit file. Your credit file may be disclosed only to someone the credit bureau believes will use the information for one or more of the following purposes:

1. Granting you credit, reviewing your account, or collecting on your account.
2. Considering you for possible employment.
3. Considering you for an insurance policy.
4. Deciding whether or not you are eligible for a license or other government-related benefits, which by law require consideration of your financial responsibility or status. A credit bureau may also disclose "identifying" information, such as your name, address, places of employment, and former places of employment,

to a government agent.

5. Furnishing information for a business transaction between you and another person (such as renting an apartment), as long as the person requesting it has a legitimate need for it.

6. Responding to a court order.

7. Responding to an Internal Revenue Service (IRS) subpoena (the IRS must notify you of the request and give you time to challenge the subpoena).

8. Your credit file may also be disclosed to someone other than yourself if you give the credit bureau written permission to do so.

Q: Why should I care about the information in my credit file?

A: The information contained in your credit file often determines whether or not you will be granted credit. It may also be used by insurance companies to decide whether to insure you or in setting your insurance rate. Often, incorrect information is entered in your file, and if this occurs, you would want to have it removed.

Q: How can I find out what information is in my credit file?

A: If you apply for credit and are rejected, or if you are denied insurance, or if the cost of your insurance increases because of information contained in a credit report, the creditor denying you credit or insurance is required by law to supply you with the name and address of the credit bureau that supplied the report.

The credit bureau is required to disclose the information they have about you free of charge if you ask for the disclosure within thirty days of being notified of your credit or insurance denial. You can get in touch with the credit bureau either in person, by letter, or by telephone to learn what is in your credit file.

If you have not been denied credit or insurance and are simply curious to know what is in your file, you can contact a credit bureau for that information, although in this case, you will have to pay a fee or service charge. You can find the names of credit bureaus in your area by looking in the Yellow Pages under the heading of "Credit Reporting Agencies." If more than one agency is listed, you should contact each one to see if it has your credit report on file.

Q: What is an investigative report and how is it different from a credit report?

A: An investigative report differs from a standard credit report in two ways:

1. It contains a different kind of information. A credit report contains information relating to your credit history and information available from public record. An investigative report deals with matters of a more personal nature such as your character, general reputation, and lifestyle;

2. The information is gathered in a different way. The information in an investigative report is obtained by personal interviews with your friends, associates and neighbors. Information in a credit report is obtained from the credit bureau and public records.

Q: For what are investigative reports used?

A: Investigative reports are used mostly by insurance companies and potential employers. Insurance companies use them in helping to determine whether you are a good insurance risk. Potential employers may use them to help decide whether they want to hire you. Your current employer may use them to assist in promotional decisions.

Q: Do I have to give my permission before an investigative report about me can be made?

A: No, but the person who requests an investigative report has three days to notify you that an investigative report has been ordered.

Q: Can I find out what information is in my investigative file?

A: Yes. You are entitled to know the "nature and substance" of all information in your investigative file. You are not entitled to know the source of information if it was gathered only for use in preparing an investigative report and used for no other purpose. You are also entitled to know who has received investigative reports about you within the past six months (or within the last two years if the report was made for employment purposes).

Q: Does the law provide any penalties for someone who willfully obtains information from a consumer reporting agency under false pretenses?

A: Yes. Anyone willfully obtaining information from a consumer reporting agency under false pretenses is subject to a maximum criminal fine of five thousand dollars and/or a maximum of one year in prison.

Q: Does the law provide any penalties for officers or employees of consumer reporting agencies who willfully provide information from the agency's files to an unauthorized person?

A: Yes. The penalties are the same as above. A maximum fine of five thousand dollars or a maximum of one year in prison or both.

Q: If a consumer believes a credit bureau has violated the law, but does not want to sue, can he complain to someone?

A: Yes. A consumer can file a complaint with the Federal Trade Commission, Attorney General, or Consumer Credit Commission.

PART TWO

FIGHTING BACK

So far, you have been made aware of how the credit bureaus gather and report information regarding your habits and lifestyle. You have learned that this information is often incorrectly reported and that you can be denied credit, insurance, and even employment because of someone else's mistakes. We now come to the question, "What can be done about it?"

On April 25, 1971, the Fair Credit Reporting Act went into effect. This little-known federal law was enacted by Congress to protect consumers against the reporting of inaccurate, misleading, or obsolete information. It was designed to ensure that consumer reporting agencies (credit bureaus) operate in a responsible and equitable manner.

The Fair Credit Reporting Act gives you the ammunition to fight back and beat the bureaucrats at their own game. It provides you with a list of rights and procedures which will assist you in clearing away negative remarks and reestablishing your creditworthiness.

Properly understanding and utilizing the Fair Credit Reporting Act will enable you to have bankruptcy, judgments, late payments, collection accounts, charge-offs, and other derogatory information permanently removed from your files.

CHAPTER NINE

HOW TO RIGHT A WRONG

The first step is to obtain copies of your credit reports from each of the major credit bureaus in your area. You can find their addresses in the Yellow Pages under Credit Reporting Agencies. If you have been denied credit within the past thirty days, you can obtain a free copy of your report by enclosing a photocopy of the denial letter along with your request. Be sure to include your full name, date of birth, Social Security number, and addresses for the past five years.

If you have not been denied credit within the last thirty days, you may still purchase a copy of your reports from each bureau. In California, the cost for a copy of your credit report is eight dollars from each of the major bureaus. The cost in other states may vary. Appendices A and B contain examples of letters used to request copies of credit reports.

You also have the right to visit the credit bureau in person in order to review your file. This can be done by calling the bureau and making an appointment. You will then need to present the proper identification and pay the required fee. The law also allows you to be accompanied by one other person of your choosing.

If you request your credit reports by mail, there is usually a waiting period of about three to four weeks before you receive copies. They will include an explanation of some of the various codes and abbreviations used. The previous sections in this book should also help you to decipher what is on your credit report.

According to the Fair Credit Reporting Act, you have the right to dispute any remark on your report which you "reasonably believe" to be inaccurate or incomplete (see Appendix C). The credit bureau, in turn, is compelled by law to reinvestigate those items within "a reasonable period of time." In most cases, a reasonable period of time has been interpreted as twenty working days. If the bureau finds that the information was incorrect, obsolete, or could no longer be verified, it must correct or delete the information.

Recently, however, the bureaus have tried to circumvent this law by sending out form letters containing such statements as, "Your dispute is frivolous and irrelevant. We therefore refuse to investigate." Or even worse, "We have reason to believe that you have been in contact with a credit repair agency. Therefore, we refuse to investigate your disputes."

Such arrogant disregard for the law by these bureaucratic hypocrites is one of the reasons this book was written. There are several remedies for such violations of your rights, which we will soon discuss in detail.

If a bureau does not respond to your initial dispute within a "reasonable time," follow up immediately with another letter (Appendix D). This time, demand that they respond to your dispute immediately and state that you will be forced to take legal action if you do not hear from them within two weeks. *Be sure to maintain copies of all correspondence.*

If the bureau persists in violating your rights by refusing to reinvestigate your dispute, send them a final letter (Appendix E). This time, send copies of your letter along with copies of the original request to the Federal Trade Commission, the Attorney General, and the Consumer Credit Commission. Now you are ready to do battle.

CHAPTER TEN

SUE THE BASTARDS

The Fair Credit Reporting Act further states that legal action can be taken against a consumer reporting agency, the user of a report, or a person furnishing report information. In other words, you have the right to sue a company for damages if it willfully or negligently violates the law and—if the suit is successful—to collect attorney's fees and court costs. The law allows such a suit on the grounds of defamation, invasion of privacy, or negligence.

This aspect of the law was demonstrated successfully in 1974 in the case of Millstone vs. O'Hanlon Reports. In this case, James Millstone's auto insurance was cancelled after the insurance company received an investigative consumer report which described Millstone as a suspected drug user. The accusation came from a former neighbor. The reporting agency refused to grant Millstone access to his records and made no attempt to verify the information. The court was outraged and referred to the bureau's methods as "slipshod and slovenly." Millstone was awarded $25,000 for punitive damages, $25,000 for actual damages, and $12,500 for costs and attorney's fees. The agency appealed on the grounds that its practices were protected by the First Amendment. The higher court upheld the decision.

The court held that consumer credit reports published by a consumer credit reporting agency and distributed for commercial purposes without regard to social concerns or grievances do not constitute speech under the protection of the First Amendment. The court further held that the consumer reporting agency's failure to disclose—at the request of the consumer—the substance and nature of its file on the consumer (as well as forcing the consumer to make several trips to its local office to obtain additional information) constituted a willful violation of the Fair Credit Reporting Act. Though the plaintiff (consumer) suffered no lost wages and incurred no medical expenses on account of injuries therein, his suffering by reason of mental anguish (including symptoms of sleeplessness and nervousness caused by the numerous times he had to contact the agency to obtain information in the file—in many instances having to leave his employment for meetings with agency personnel) entitled him to actual damages, punitive damages, and an allowance for an attorney's fee.

In the case of Serino vs. Dun & Bradstreet, the court made the following ruling: "When a credit reporting agency undertook to publish credit information about a woman, it was incumbent upon it to exercise due care in obtaining and publishing credit information about her, and justice demands the imposition of liability for damages resulting proximately from its negligent breach of such duty."

Rejecting the contention that reports of a mercantile agency (credit bureau) to its patrons on the financial standing of business concerns are privileged, the court, in Pacific Packing Co. vs. Bradstreet Co. said, "The only safe and just rule either in law or morals is the one that exacts truthfulness in business as well as elsewhere and places a penalty upon falsehood, making it dangerous for a mercantile, commercial, or any other agency to sell and traffic falsehood and misrepresentation about the standing and credit of men or corporations . . . . If a mercantile agency can safely make false reports about the financial standing and credit of the citizen and destroy his business, it can then take the next step with equal impunity and destroy his reputation, leaving him shorn and helpless."

The following ruling is from a more recent case:

Case Number SC60071

Notice of Ruling and Judgment

Based on the evidence, the court finds for the Plaintiffs and orders that judgment be entered against Defendant TRW Information Services in the amount of $500 plus court costs and filing fees as shown by the court records. Although defendant is correct that the inaccuracies in defendant's credit report were not the sole reason that credit was refused on two occasions so as to entitle plaintiffs to recover total damages claimed, those inaccuracies did cause plaintiffs to incur out-of-pocket expenses in excess of $120 and to experience mental suffering and stress in order to refute the misrepresentations as to their *financial history and cause defendant to delete them from future reports. Defendant is engaged in the business of furnishing credit reports and charges a fee for such services. In publishing data which damages the credit standing of the persons named in the report, defendant cannot claim immunity simply because they obtain the basic data from another source. The republication of false data creates an independent grounds for liability.*

Dated: July 25, 1988

/S/ Harold Johnson, Municipal Court Judge

There have, subsequently, been other successful lawsuits brought against consumer reporting agencies. Such battles are not easily won, however. Victories are based upon the determination of "willful noncompliance" or "negligent noncompliance" according to Fair Credit Reporting Act requirements. If *willful* noncompliance is determined, the injured party may be awarded actual damages, punitive damages, court costs, and attorney's fees. For *negligent* noncompliance, the court may only award actual damages, costs, and attorney's fees. In cases of negligent noncompliance, the credit bureau will often use a defense based upon "reasonable procedures." By demonstrating a "good faith effort," the bureau is often able to circumvent this legally undefined area. The key to victory, therefore, is to prove that the credit bureau was willfully noncompliant with Fair Credit Reporting Act requirements.

There is a two-year statute of limitations on filing a civil suit under the Fair Credit Reporting Act. If, however, a credit bureau or report user has willfully misrepresented information, and when that information is relevant to the case against the bureau or user, the two-year period does not commence until the date the misrepresentation was discovered.

If a credit bureau violates your rights under the Fair Credit Reporting Act by claiming that your dispute is "frivolous and irrelevant," you have the right to file a lawsuit against them. In some cases, such legal action may take up to several years before trial. In the meantime, your attorney may file a motion for injunctive relief. This is a formal request to the court to grant a temporary order restraining the credit bureau from including the disputed items in your credit reports until the case is resolved. Since the derogatory items on your report may threaten your basic living such as your ability to write a check, rent an apartment, obtain loans, or gain employment, the court may be willing to grant such a motion. If the motion is granted, the credit bureau must refrain from including the disputed information in your credit reports.

It is also possible to file a complaint against the credit bureau in the small claims court. In California, the filing fee is only six dollars, and the limit on such claims is two thousand dollars. Neither party may be represented in court by an attorney. You may, however, consult with an attorney for advice before your hearing. You may also consult with small claims advisors. If more consumers begin to take this type of legal action, it may create an incentive for the credit bureaus to start obeying the law and investigate the dispute instead of trying to avoid their responsibility under the Fair Credit Reporting Act.

If enough people got together, it would be possible to file a class action suit against the credit bureaus. Such an action would begin by gathering together a group of consumers who have received letters from a certain credit bureau refusing to investigate their disputes. Filing a class action suit against a major credit bureau would put a serious dent in the bureaucratic machinery. Class action suits have often resulted in awards of several million dollars.

If you have any intention of taking legal action against a credit bureau, it is important that you maintain copies of all of your correspondence with the bureau as well as with any credit grantors who have denied you credit. The key to winning a lawsuit is documented evidence. Good record keeping is essential.

The following is a summary of your legal rights under the Fair Credit Reporting Act. For a complete reproduction of the Act, see Appendix F.

YOUR RIGHTS UNDER THE FAIR CREDIT REPORTING ACT

1. To be told the nature and sources of the information collected about you by a credit bureau.

2. To obtain this information free of charge when you have been denied credit, insurance, or employment within thirty days. Otherwise, the reporting agency can charge a reasonable fee for the disclosure.

3. To take anyone of your choosing with you when you visit the credit bureau.

4. To be told who has received a credit report on you within the preceding six months, or within the preceding two years if the report was furnished for employment purposes.

5. To have incomplete, incorrect, or obsolete information reinvestigated and, if found to be inaccurate or impossible to verify, to have such information removed from your file.

6. When a dispute between you and the credit bureau cannot be resolved, to have your version of

the dispute placed in the file and included in future reports.

7. To request that the credit bureau send your consumer statement to all future credit grantors.

8. To have a credit report withheld from anyone who does not have a legitimate business need for the information.

9. To sue a company for damages if it willingly or negligently violates the law and—if the suit is successful—to collect attorney's fees and court costs.

10. To be notified if a company is requesting an investigative consumer report.

11. To request that any company that ordered an investigative report provide further information as to the nature and scope of the investigation.

12. To have negative information removed from your report after seven years. One major exception is bankruptcy, which may be reported for ten years.

THE FEDERAL TRADE COMMISSION

The Federal Trade Commission is the agency responsible for enforcing the Fair Credit Reporting Act. If a credit bureau has violated your rights under this law, you can file a complaint with the nearest regional office. Address your inquiries to "Director."

Headquarters:
Federal Trade Commission
Pennsylvania Avenue &
Sixth Street, N.W.
Washington, D.C. 20580
(202) 523-3830

Regional Offices:
1718 Peachtree St., N.W.
Suite 1000
Atlanta, GA 30367

150 Causeway St., Rm. 1301
Boston, MA 02114

118 St. Clair Ave., Suite 500
Cleveland, OH 44114

20001 Bryan St., Suite 2665
Dallas, TX 75201

11000 Wilshire Blvd.
Los Angeles, CA 90024

1405 Curtis St., Suite 2900
Denver, CO 80202

26 Federal Plaza, Rm. 2243-EB
New York, NY 10278

450 Golden Gate Ave.
San Francisco, CA 94102

912 2nd Ave., 28th Floor
Seattle, WA 98174

The following are some of the Federal Trade Commission's recommendations and interpretations regarding the Fair Credit Reporting Act.

TIME RESTRICTIONS

• There is no time restriction in reporting of information that is not adverse.
• The act does not require consumer reporting agencies to report adverse information for the time periods set forth, but prohibits them from reporting adverse items beyond those time periods.
• The date that the consumer reporting agency

acquired the adverse information is irrelevant to the length of time for which that information may be reported.

• If a tax lien (or other lien) remains unsatisfied, it may be reported as long as it remains filed against the consumer, without limitation, because this subsection addresses only paid tax liens.

FRIVOLOUS AND IRRELEVANT

The mere presence of contradictory information in the file does not provide the consumer reporting agency "reasonable grounds to believe that the dispute by the consumer is frivolous or irrelevant." A consumer reporting agency must assume a consumer's dispute is bona fide unless there is clear and convincing evidence to the contrary. Such evidence may consist of letters from consumers disputing all information in their files without providing any allegations concerning specific items. The agency is not required to complete a reinvestigation of one it has just conducted simply because the consumer reiterates a dispute about the same item of information.

DISPUTE STATEMENTS

A consumer who disputes multiple items of information in his file may insert a one hundred-word statement in regard to each disputed item.

CHAPTER TWELVE

THE TRUTH ABOUT CREDIT REPAIR

In 1971, only 10 percent of TRW's computerized credit files contained negative information. Today that figure is closer to 70 percent. Much of this negative data is incorrect, misleading, or obsolete. As a result, many innocent citizens have been treated unfairly. This has led to a legitimate need for someone to intercede on their behalf.

In recent years, we have seen the emergence of a new industry. Commonly known as Credit Clinics, Credit Repair Agencies, or Credit Service Companies, these organizations claim that they will help you to correct your credit record, improve your credit standing, or obtain credit cards and loans. Their fees range from one hundred dollars to as high as three thousand dollars, depending on the type of service to be performed.

In response to a definite need, the professional credit consultant has emerged as a modern-day dragon slayer. By properly understanding and utilizing the Fair Credit Reporting Act and other consumer protection laws, the legitimate credit consultant is able to guide the consumer through the computerized web of this cashless society. Second-class citizens have been transformed miraculously into creditworthy individuals by these high-tech consumer advocates who dare to challenge a system that considers itself to be above the law.

This unique group of entrepreneurs has become the target of a well-staged media attack. This carefully orchestrated conspiracy has been designed to destroy credibility, develop strict legislation prohibiting such activities, and put the credit clinics out of business. Press releases have been sent strategically to major media publications across the country. Articles have been printed which detailed horror stories of rip-offs by swindlers posing as credit consultants. As a result, we have seen the concept of "credit repair" made synonymous with consumer fraud.

There are crooks in every profession. The credit consulting field is by no means immune to such problems as incompetence and dishonesty. Neither are the fields of journalism, politics, law, or medicine. None of the other professions, however, has been under the massive guns of such corporate giants as TRW, Trans Union, and CBI/Equifax.

The majority of adult American consumers are in need of a credit consultant's services, but how can they be helped when they have been brainwashed into helplessness? Big Brother would like you to remain paralyzed by the fear of being ripped off. They would like you to continue believing that you should be condemned to a second-class existence because of a previous mistake. They would rather have you remain ignorant of the law than have you exercise your rights as a free citizen. They would rather put every credit consultant out of business than have their integrity questioned. How dare we question their integrity?

Consider the tone of the following letter from TRW to a consumer:

Dear Mr. Winston Smith:

We have received your recent correspondence.

It appears that you have been in contact with a credit repair agency.
California law states that a credit repair agency is any credit service which provides the following service:
1. improving a buyer's credit record, history or rating.
2. obtaining an extension of credit for a buyer
3. providing advice or assistance to a buyer regarding the above

It is illegal for a credit service agency to advise you to make any statement which is untrue or misleading to a credit reporting agency or credit grantor.

Due to the nature and manner in which you are commenting on your disclosure, we will not honor your request for reinvestigation as it appears to be frivolous.

Sincerely,

Joe Big Brother
Consumer Relations

Here is a follow-up letter which TRW sent out after Mr. Smith persisted in his dispute:

Dear Mr. Smith:

We have received your recent correspondence. Based on our experience concerning credit repair service procedures, your communications with TRW strongly indicate that you have been working with a credit repair agency.

We therefore again deny your request for reinvestigation, as it appears to be frivolous.

Sincerely,

Joe Big Brother
Consumer Relations

Another consumer received the following response from TRW after persistently requesting that they remove a Checkpoint from his credit report:

Dear Mr. Davies:

We are in receipt of your recent request.

Based on our experience, we have reason to believe that you have been assisted by a third party in submitting disputes. Contrary to what you may have been advised, no one can require a credit bureau to delete an accurate item of information from your file; no one can repair your credit.

In reviewing the file, we have taken into consideration the source and/or form of the dispute and believe that it is irrelevant or frivolous. Therefore, we are advising you that at this time we are not performing a reinvestigation.

Sincerely,

TRW Consumer Relations

Here is a letter received by a consumer who wrote to TRW's legal department after having been ignored by the Consumer Relations Department:

March 28, 1989
Re: Your Credit File

This is in response to the copies of your previous letters to TRW's Orange offices which you have forwarded to me.

If you believe that TRW will conduct a reinvestigation of your disputes which it has reason to believe are frivolous or irrelevant if you write enough letters to enough people, you are mistaken.

From your correspondence, it appears you have been in contact with a credit repair firm, or have purchased a "kit" which has advised you on how to "clean up" your credit file. Let me assure you that TRW has no intention of failing to properly serve its subscribers, and that all the information that properly belongs to you will be accurately reported. Whoever has advised you that TRW has to "prove" to you items of information is mistaken.

Very truly yours,

Harry I. Howard
Senior Counsel (TRW)

Trans Union has come up with an even stronger approach. Consider the tone of the following letter to a consumer:

Dear Miss Gullible:

Recently we received correspondence from a third party concerning your credit profile.

Due to the confidential nature of the information in your report, we are unable to recognize this third party.

If you would like to receive a current copy of your credit profile, you may dial 645-6000 for complete instructions.

If you used the services of a "credit clinic" and they assisted you in requesting this disclosure, and you paid a sizeable fee for this service, you may be interested to know that government agencies are investigating "credit clinics," which may be charging high fees and otherwise deceiving consumers.

If you have reason to believe that the fee charged by the "credit clinic" was too high or its services were misrepresented, and you would like to assist in the investigation, please let us know. With your permission, we will provide the information to the appropriate authorities conducting the investigation.

It is our practice to do everything possible to assist consumers in understanding the information which is contained in their files, and to make sure that the information contained therein is current and accurate.

Please let me know if I may assist you in any

way. I may be reached at 645-1848.

Sincerely,

David C. Hendershot
Operations Manager
Trans Union Credit Information Co.
Chicago Division

The following is a letter from Trans Union to members of the Merchants Association:

March 1, 1989

TO: Members of Merchants Association

The integrity of credit history information is under attack by credit clinics throughout the country. No doubt you have seen the advertisements guaranteeing "to erase bad credit" and have wondered how it can be done. Bad credit can only be erased if you, the credit grantor, allow it to be done.

Credit clinics advise consumers to challenge the accuracy of every adverse item of information in the file in the hope that you, the credit grantor, will not respond to a reverification request within a reasonable period of time. Failure to respond forces the credit bureau to delete the adverse item in compliance with the Fair Credit Reporting Act. When this happens, the credit clinic wins. Good customers and other credit grantors are the losers.

Another credit clinic scheme is to "negotiate" payment of the adverse account with the credit grantor in return for a "favorable report" or "no rating" to the credit bureau. This form of blackmail also undermines the integrity of the credit information and makes a winner out of the credit clinic.

We are confident that you support and depend on accurate credit history information. The enclosed statement on integrity of credit information has the approval and support of the national Credit Grantor Advisory Group sponsored by our trade association, Associated Credit Bureaus, Inc. Please indicate your support by completing and returning the attached policy statement.

Finally, please take a moment to ask your credit department how it is processing requests for reverification of adverse information from the credit bureau. Also, have contacts been received requesting the removal of adverse information if an account is paid in full? On the reverse side of this letter is the verification form that we use to confirm information in our file. If you learn that you are inadvertently contributing to the success of the credit clinics, please instruct your personnel on the proper handling of these requests. Together we will assure the continued integrity of the credit file.

Sincerely,

Larry D. Wages
General Manager (Trans Union)

POLICY STATEMENT ON INTEGRITY OF CREDIT INFORMATION

Recognizing that the integrity and effective functioning of the consumer credit system is dependent upon the furnishing, maintaining, and reporting of factual credit history information, which is a responsibility shared by credit grantors and consumer reporting agencies alike, our company reaffirms:

1. That consumer credit history information will be reported in a factual, precise and objective manner.

2. That requests by consumers for reverification of challenged information will be processed promptly.

3. That upon the request of a consumer, we will promptly review that consumer's account, disclosing to the consumer the factual payment record as reported to consumer reporting agencies and/or to other creditors.

4. That unless an error is discovered, the consumer will be advised that the factual credit history information will continue to be reported.

Here is a response to that letter, written by Mr. Ken Yarbrough, Executive Director of the Consumer Credit Commission:

Consumer Credit Commission
4286 Redwood Highway, #350
San Rafael, CA 94903
415-491-4152

On March 17, 1989, a request was received to initiate a staff opinion relevant to the Trans Union letter placed on the reverse side of this document. Pursuant to that request, the following findings are hereby presented:

The commission has found no evidence which indicates that factual credit history information is under attack by credit clinics throughout the country. Nor has the commission found substantiating evidence indicating that the credit grantor is negligent in his duties, as indicated.

The commission has published a report and has

identified the actions associated with a "disputory cycle" as an "UNJUST CREDIT PRACTICE." Any credit repair firm found to be in violation will be reported to appropriate authorities. However, evidence reveals that when disputed information is not returned in a timely manner and under the law must be deleted, it may again be added to the file as soon as it is received, because it is treated as "new" information. The urgency in this regard is then somewhat reduced.

Additionally, the commission is not aware of conditions whereby the "credit clinic wins" or where "good customers and other credit grantors are the losers." The law in this regard is exact. Information (either positive or negative) which is found to be inaccurate or can no longer be verified must be promptly deleted from the file. The deletion of nonverifiable information, either negative or positive, is an asset to the credit community and the consumer to whom it relates, and it is in direct compliance with the law.

Negotiation of contractual items is a basic principle of business. The commission is of the staff opinion that negotiated items are not a form of "blackmail" as indicated in the letter. Further, the commission supports the basic rights of individuals and business firms when related to compromised agreement. The commission is aware of a $3.2 million judgment recently awarded a consumer against a major bank. Effective negotiations early in this event may very well have resulted in a favorable settlement, in that the actual dollar damage amounted to only $2,000.

America's entire judicial system supports the

usage of the negotiated settlement and compromised agreement. Numerous lawsuits have
been halted or avoided entirely through negotiated settlements. States have enacted legislation which favors compromised agreements,
and many industries routinely depend upon
negotiation as their primary means of conducting business.

Traffic schools educate infraction violators relevant to traffic safety. Upon completion (as a
negotiated settlement), adverse traffic history
is promptly deleted from the offender's official
record. The commission thus supports the use
of negotiation and compromised agreement
between the creditor and consumer.

The commission does not visualize the making
of a "winner" of a credit clinic simply because
the credit grantor agrees to a negotiated settlement. The integrity and effective functioning
of the consumer credit system is:

1. Creation of a consumer reporting agency
which integrates and fully verifies information
received from credit bureaus, credit grantors,
and the consumer to whom it relates; and provides a certified consumer report.
2. Credit grantor education as it relates to
creditworthiness and interpretations of consumer reports.
3. Detailed education programs concerning
consumer budgeting procedures, long-term,
intermediate, and immediate financial goals,
and consumer credit rights.
4. The production of a detailed consumer
financial plan to include a strategy for savings, investments, and charity, as well as a
strategy for the acquisition of major purchases
that must be financed, such as automobiles,

real estate, and so on.

It is in this regard that the commission recommends against the adoption of a policy which limits opportunities for compromise between consumers and credit grantors and finds that these situations are better handled on a case-by-case basis.

Respectfully submitted,

Ken Yarbrough
Executive Director

TRW and Trans Union have also been putting the pressure on the small independent credit bureaus. They put several of these small bureaus out of business completely when it was learned that credit reports had been supplied to credit repair agencies. On one occasion an agency was told that it could not order any more credit reports from a particular bureau until it signed the following agreement:

I _____ *am affiliated with* _____. *I/We are not a "credit clean-up" service. I also understand that my membership fee is nonrefundable.*

*DATE:*_____
*Signature*_____
*DATE:*_____
*Signature*_____
Credit Bureau Manager

It's reminiscent of the McCarthy era, when people were asked routinely, "Are you now, or have you ever been, a member of the Communist Party?"

In some areas, the situation is getting so bad

that credit consultants are going over to "the other side" and betraying their former associates. One such instance involved a prominent consultant in Seattle, Washington, who called himself "The Credit Doctor." When a client recently came to him for assistance, he turned her away, replying arrogantly, "Oh, I don't have to do credit repair anymore."

"What do you mean?" she inquired.

"I just made a deal with CBI (Equifax)," he replied. "I showed them a way to put all of the credit clinics out of business for good, and they paid me enough money to retire on."

CHAPTER THIRTEEN

1984 REVISITED

In the prophetic year of 1984, TRW successfully lobbied for a California law requiring credit service companies to adhere to a strict set of bonding requirements and regulatory restrictions. This law was known as the Credit Services Act of 1984. Similar laws have been enacted in a majority of states.

The "stated" purposes of the act are to provide prospective clients of credit services organizations with the information necessary to make intelligent decisions regarding the purchase of those services and to protect the public from unfair or deceptive advertising and business practices.

The truth, however, is that the act was designed specifically to put the credit repair companies out of business—once and for all. The common opinion among consultants is that the bonding and contractual requirements place undue hardship upon the consultant's ability to function effectively for the client. Many are even of the opinion that the act is unconstitutional in that it places severe restrictions upon the free speech of individuals. As a result of the act, many credit repair agencies have either gone out of business completely or have gone "underground" by incorporating their credit consulting into another form of business, such as real estate, financial planning, or auto brokering. Others have simply ceased advertising and relied upon word of mouth to generate new clientele.

According to the Credit Services Act of 1984, a credit services organization consists of anyone who provides any of the following services:

1. Improving a buyer's credit record, history or rating.

2. Obtaining an extension of credit for a buyer.

3. Providing advice or assistance to a buyer regarding the above.

These regulations do not apply to:

• Regulated financial institutions (for example, mortgage or loan companies).

• Banks and savings and loan associations whose accounts or deposits are eligible for federal deposit insurance.

• Nonprofit, tax-exempt organizations.

• Prorators (people licensed by the California Department of Corporations who—for a fee—receive money from debtors and distribute it in payment to creditors).

• Real estate brokers licensed by the California Department of Real Estate.

- Attorneys.
- Brokers or dealers registered with the Securities and Exchange Commission or the Commodity Futures Trading Commission.

The credit services agency must provide the consumer with a written contract that contains:

- A complete description of the services to be performed.
- Any guarantees or promises about refunds.
- The date by which the services will be performed.
- The agency's name and principal business address and the name of a responsible agency representative.
- All terms and conditions of payment.
- A disclosure statement describing your right to cancel the contract within five days for any reason. The contract must be accompanied by a "Notice of Cancellation" form detailing the five-day cancellation rights and must contain a blank cancellation form.

The credit services agency must also provide the consumer with a written description containing:

- Information about the agency's trust account or bond.
- Complete information about your legal rights to review your credit record and to dispute the accuracy of items in the report.
- The approximate price that will be charged for a credit report. If a consumer cancels the contract, the agency must return the deposit within fifteen days of the cancellation date.

Credit service agencies must also obtain a surety bond or establish a trust account for five thousand dollars or 5 percent of the total fees charged during the previous twelve months (to a maximum of twenty-five thousand dollars). If a credit services agency fails to provide the promised services, these funds will be used to reimburse the consumer.

It is illegal for an agency to charge money for referrals to retail sellers to which a person could apply directly for credit. Also, agencies may not make untrue or misleading statements to any credit reporting bureau or agency about an individual's credit standing or capacity or advise an individual to make such statements.

Violation of any of these provisions is a misdemeanor, punishable under local and state laws. The agency is also vulnerable to lawsuits in small claims court or municipal court, depending upon the amount of monetary damages claims. A consumer who files suit against a credit service agency can claim damages plus attorney's fees and costs.

In 1987, Representative Frank Annunzio of Illinois introduced HR 458, a bill to regulate the credit repair industry. The bill did not pass in the 1987 session of Congress but was reintroduced in 1988. HR 458 sets forth the following guidelines for credit repair agencies:

1. Requires all credit repair agencies to procure a surety bond of fifty thousand dollars before they can receive compensation for their services; or, if they do not have a bond, to wait until completion of services before they can receive compensation.

2. Prohibits credit repair consultants from advising their clients to make any statement that is untrue or misleading.

3. Requires a written contract/retaining agreement that spells out clearly the amount of fee charged, the description of services to be performed by the credit repair consultant, including all guarantees and all promises of full or partial refunds, and the estimated length of time for performing the services. Included in the contract will be a mandato-

ry clause stating the client's right to cancel the contract at anytime prior to midnight of the third day
after the date of transaction.

CHAPTER FOURTEEN

CONSUMER CREDIT COMMISSION

The Consumer Credit Commission was founded to provide credit protection and financial education to consumers. Membership in the commission calls for businesses and consumers to agree to the following Code of Ethics:

• To conduct all business dealings in an ethical and legal manner

• To support a combined effort against unethical conduct in the consumer credit industry

• To promote creditworthiness to the public through the support of sound and responsible financial management and consumer education programs

The following Credit and Financial Consultant's Creed

was created in an effort to restore credibility in the credit and financial field:

To do business together effectively, we must respect and value one another. It is important to you to know how we think, how we do business, and how we approach our relationship with you, the consumer.

The end and purpose of business is profit. A business person, then, would presumably place that above all else. We recognize, however, human values to be far superior, and therefore, they modify our pursuit of profit.

It is our contention that no one need earn a dollar at someone else's expense. Thus we eschew all gimmicks and turn to complete openness and honesty in our relationships with clients.

What we recommend to a client is precisely what we ourselves would do were we in their position with our knowledge.

The Consumer Credit Commission recommends to all consumers who are seeking the advice and assistance of credit consultants to seek wisely. Check with the commission to determine if previous complaints have been filed. They can also assist you in locating a competent credit consultant in your area.

The commission has recently adopted a policy of "Zero Tolerance." All complaints of fraud, misrepresentation and unjust credit practices will be aggressively pursued by a Special Pursuit Team. Disclosed violations will be reported to the Federal Trade Commission, Postal Inspector, appropriate State Attorney General, Consumer Affairs authorities, Secretary of State, District Attorney, and local police. Appropriate notices will be sent to advertising media, and a concerted effort will be made for injunctive and civil relief.

CHAPTER FIFTEEN

QUESTIONS AND ANSWERS

Q: Is it really possible to "erase bad credit"?

A: Yes. Through the proper understanding and utilization of the Fair Credit Reporting Act, it is possible to have negative items reinvestigated and—if found to be inaccurate, obsolete, or impossible to verify —corrected or deleted.

Q: Isn't it true that credit consultants can do nothing for a consumer that he can't do himself for free?

A: You can file bankruptcy or divorce without a lawyer. You can also overhaul your transmission without the help of a mechanic. However, most people don't have the time or interest to attain expertise in every field. So, of course, you can buy a book on credit repair and do it yourself, or you can enlist the services of a professional.

Q: What if I want to clean up my own credit?

A: Start by ordering copies of your credit reports. Then follow the procedures outlined earlier in this book.

Q: How can I get copies of my credit reports without having to wait three or four weeks?

A: Some credit consultants and independent credit bureaus can FAX a copy of your report the same day you request them.

Q: You mentioned that some consultants are helping people to "start over" with a new credit file. How is this possible?

A: By understanding the file identification systems of each of the major credit bureaus, it is possible to circumvent those systems and "start over" with a new credit file. This new credit file will have no connection to your old file but will simply read, "NO RECORD FOUND." It is then possible to re-establish credit on the new file utilizing a variety of strategies. This method is thoroughly detailed in my previous book, *Credit Secrets: How to Erase Bad Credit*, available from Paladin Press.

Q: What advice would you give to a person who would like to become a professional credit consultant?

A: Make sure you have your bases covered before hanging out your shingle. Obtain the necessary bonding and licensing requirements. Most important, make sure you know what you're talking about before you start giving out advice. Read every book you can find on the subject of credit and consumer law.

Q: What do you foresee for the credit repair industry?

A: As more people fall victim to Big Brother and his bureaucrats, we will see an ever-increasing need for the services of a professional "dragon-slayer." The credit repair industry is an idea whose time has come. It is definitely here to stay.

Q: Don't credit repair consultants worry that the credit bureaus will try to sue them for libel or defamation of character?

A: Truth is the best defense.

CONCLUSION

 George Orwell once described what he and others were trying to accomplish in their exposés of the evils of modern political developments in these words:

"Some of these are imaginative writers, some not, but they are all alike in that they are trying to write contemporary history, but unofficial history, the kind that is ignored in the textbooks and lied about in the newspapers."
—From Orwell's essay,
Arthur Koestler

In a like manner, this book will serve to record an aspect of contemporary history which might have otherwise gone unreported. I realize that the issues which have been discussed may produce strong reactions from certain individuals, especially those who are reading it from seats of power. The truth owes no apologies, however, and will—despite all obstacles—prevail. My hope is that at least a few brave souls have become enlightened.

NOTABLE QUOTATIONS

"As every man goes through life he fills in a number of forms for the the record, each containing a number of questions . . . There are thus hundreds of little threads in all. If these threads were suddenly to become visible, the whole sky would look like a spider's web; and if they materialized as rubber, trams, buses, trains, and even people would all lose the ability to move; and the wind would be unable to carry torn-up newspapers or autumn leaves along the streets of the city. They are not visible; they are not material; but every man is constantly aware of their existence."

—Alexander Solzhenitsyn
Cancer Ward

"They tell us, sir, that we are weak—unable to cope with so formidable an adversary. But when shall we be stronger? Will it be when we are totally disarmed?

"Shall we gather strength by irresolution and inaction? Shall we acquire the means of effectual resistance by lying supinely on our backs and hugging the delusive phantom of hope, until our enemies shall have bound us hand and foot?

"Sir, we shall not fight our battle alone. There is a just God who presides over the destinies of nations . . . The battle, sir, is not to the strong alone; it is to the vigilant, the active, the brave . . . There is no retreat but in submission and slavery! Our chains are forged!

"Gentlemen may cry, 'Peace, Peace!' but there is no peace. The war is actually begun! . . . Why stand we here idle? What would they have? Is life so dear, or peace so sweet, as to be purchased at the price of chains and slavery? Forbid it, Almighty God! I know not what course others may take; but as for me, give me liberty or give me death."

—Patrick Henry
House of Burgesses,
Virginia, March 1775

"And ye shall know the truth. And the truth shall make you free."

—Jesus of Nazareth
John 8:32

PART THREE

APPENDICES

REQUEST FOR REPORT (AFTER DENIAL)

Date
Name of Credit Bureau
Address of Credit Bureau

To Whom It May Concern:

I have been denied credit within the past thirty days by _____, based on a credit report from your company. Enclosed is a copy of the denial letter. Please send me a copy of my credit report as soon as possible.

NAME
PRESENT ADDRESS
PREVIOUS ADDRESS
SOCIAL SECURITY #
DATE OF BIRTH

Thank you very much for your immediate attention.

Sincerely yours,

Your Name

REQUEST FOR REPORT (NO DENIAL)

Date
Name of Credit Bureau
Address of Credit Bureau

To Whom It May Concern:

Enclosed is a check for $_____ to cover the indicated cost of providing me with a copy of my credit report. Please send the credit report as soon as possible to the name and address below:

NAME
PRESENT ADDRESS
PREVIOUS ADDRESS
SOCIAL SECURITY #
DATE OF BIRTH

Thank you very much for your immediate attention.

Sincerely yours,

Your Name

SAMPLE DISPUTE LETTER

123 Hardluck St.
Credit Card, CA 90000

July 4, 1990

The Report's Wrong
Information Service
1313 Babylon Road
Bureaucrat, MI 44444

ATTN: Consumer Relations

I formally request that the following items be immediately investigated. I would like them removed in order to show my true credit history, as these items should not be on my report. They are injurious to my credit history since they are inaccurate.

Company Name   Account #   Comments

I would also like to point out that the following credit inquiries were never authorized by me:

Company Name   Subscriber #   Date of Inquiry

Please complete your investigation and send me my updated credit report.

Thank you for your time and consideration.

Sincerely yours,

Winston Smith
SSN: 123-45-6789
DOB: 5-5-55

FOLLOW-UP TO A DISPUTE

Date

Name of Credit Bureau
Address of Credit Bureau
Attn: Consumer Relations Department

Dear _____:

On _____ (date of first dispute), I sent you a request to investigate certain items on my credit report that I believe to be incorrect or inaccurate. But as of today, six weeks have passed and I have not yet received a response from you.

Under the Fair Credit Reporting Act, you are required to respond within "a reasonable time." If the information cannot be verified, please delete it from my credit report.

I would appreciate your immediate attention to this matter and your informing me of the result.

Yours sincerely,

Your Name
Address
SSN #
DOB

SECOND FOLLOW-UP LETTER

Date

Name of Bureau
Address
City, State, ZIP

Re: Your name
Address
SSN#

To Whom It May Concern:

Four weeks ago, I sent you a follow-up letter stating that you had not responded to or investigated my disputes of incorrect items on my credit report. Copies of that letter and the original dispute letter are enclosed.

To date, you still have not complied with your obligation under the Fair Credit Reporting Act, which requires your company to ensure the correctness of reported information. I hereby demand that you immediately remove the disputed items from my credit file based on the fact that they are either inaccurate or cannot be verified. I also expect you to send me an updated copy of my credit report immediately afterward.

If I do not receive your response within the next two weeks, I will file a complaint with the Federal Trade

Commission and the Attorney General. In addition, I will not hesitate to retain my attorney to pursue my right to recover damages under the Fair Credit Reporting Act.

Please also forward me the names and addresses of individuals you contacted to verify the information so I may follow up. Thank you for your immediate attention to this matter.

Sincerely yours,

Your Name

RECOMMENDED READING

Credit Secrets: How to Erase Bad Credit. Bob Hammond, Paladin Press, P.O. Box 1307, Boulder, CO 80306.

Directory of Consumer Credit Services. Fresh Start Financial Services, 249 N Brand Blvd., Suite 376, Glendale, CA 91203.

Credit! (1987 Edition Revised by Cathy Clark). Eden Press, P.O. Box 8410, Fountain Valley, CA 92708.

Privacy! How to Get It . . . How to Enjoy It. Bill Kaysing, Eden Press, P.O. Box 8410, Fountain Valley, CA 92718.

Give Yourself Credit (Guide to Consumer Credit Laws). Subcommittee on Consumer Affairs and Coinage of the Committee on Banking, Finance, and Urban Affairs, Rm. 212, House Office Bldg., Annex No. 1, Washington, D.C. 20515.

1984. George Orwell, Harcourt Brace & World, Inc., 757 Third Avenue, New York, NY 10017.

THE FAIR CREDIT REPORTING ACT

APPENDIX I
FAIR CREDIT REPORTING ACT

*TITLE VI—PROVISIONS RELATING TO CREDIT
REPORTING AGENCIES*

AMENDMENT OF CONSUMER CREDIT PROTECTION ACT

*SEC. 601. The Consumer Credit Protection Act is amended
by adding at the end thereof the following new title:*

TITLE VI—CONSUMER CREDIT REPORTING

Sec. 601. Short title
This title may be cited as the Fair Credit Reporting Act.

Sec. 602. Findings and purpose
(a) The Congress makes the following findings:

*(1) The banking system is dependent upon fair and
accurate credit reporting. Inaccurate credit reports directly
impair the efficiency of the banking system, and unfair
credit reporting methods undermine the public confidence
which is essential to the continued functioning of the
banking system.*

*(2) An elaborate mechanism has been developed
for investigating and evaluating the creditworthiness,
credit standing, credit capacity, character, and general
reputation of consumers.*

(3) Consumer reporting agencies have assumed a

vital role in assembling and evaluating consumer credit and other information on consumers.

(4) There is a need to insure that consumer reporting agencies exercise their grave responsibilities with fairness, impartiality, and a respect for the consumer's right to privacy.

(b) It is the purpose of this title to require that consumer reporting agencies adopt reasonable procedures for meeting the need of commerce for consumer credit, personnel, insurance, and other information in a manner which is fair and equitable to the consumer with regard to the confidentiality, accuracy, relevancy, and proper utilization of such information in accordance with the requirements of this title.

Sec. 603. Definitions and rules of construction

(a) Definitions and rules of construction set forth in this section are applicable for the purposes of this title.

(b) The term "person" means any individual, partnership, corporation, trust, estate, cooperative, association, government or governmental subdivision or agency, or other entity.

(c) The term "consumer" means an individual.

(d) The term "consumer report" means any written, oral, or other communication of any information by a consumer reporting agency bearing on a consumer's creditworthiness, credit standing, credit capacity, character, general reputation, personal characteristics, or mode of living which is used or expected to be used or collected in whole or in part for the purpose of serving as a factor in establishing the consumer's eligibility for (1) credit or insurance to be used primarily for personal, family, or household purposes, or (2) employment purposes, or (3) other purposes authorized under section 604. The term does not include (A) any report containing information solely as to transactions or experiences between the consumer and the person making the report; (B) any authorization or approval of a specific extension of credit directly or indirectly by the issuer of a credit card or similar device; or (C) any report in which a person who has

been requested by a third party to make a specific extension of credit directly or indirectly to a consumer conveys his decision with respect to such request, if the third party advises the consumer of the name and address of the person to whom the request was made and such person makes the disclosures to the consumer required under section 615.

(e) The term "investigative consumer report" means a consumer report or portion thereof in which information on a consumer's character, general reputation, personal characteristics, or mode of living is obtained through personal interviews with neighbors, friends, or associates of the consumer reported on or with others with whom he is acquainted or who may have knowledge concerning any such items of information. However, such information shall not include specific factual information on a consumer's credit record obtained directly from a creditor of the consumer or from the consumer.

(f) The term "consumer reporting agency" means any person which, for monetary fees, dues, or on a cooperative nonprofit basis, regularly engages in whole or part in the practice of assembling or evaluating consumer credit information or other information on consumers for the purpose of furnishing consumer reports to third parties, and which uses any means or facility of interstate commerce for the purpose of preparing or furnishing consumer reports.

(g) The term "file," when used in connection with information on any consumer, means all of the information on that consumer recorded and retained by a consumer reporting agency, regardless of how the information is stored.

(h) The term "employment purposes," when used in connection with a consumer report, means a report used for the purpose of evaluating a consumer for employment, promotion, reassignment or retention as an employee.

(i) The term "medical information" means information or records obtained, with the consent of the individual to whom it relates, from licensed physicians or medical practitioners, hospitals, clinics, or other medical or medically related facilities.

Sec. 604. Permissible purposes of reports

A consumer reporting agency may furnish a consumer report under the following circumstances and no other:

(1) In response to the order of a court having jurisdiction to issue such an order.

(2) In accordance with the written instructions of the consumer to whom it relates.

(3) To a person which it has reason to believe—

(A) intends to use the information in connection with a credit transaction involving the consumer on whom the information is to be furnished and involving the extension of credit to, or review or collection of an account of the consumer; or

(B) intends to use the information for employment purposes; or

(C) intends to use the information in connection with the underwriting of insurance involving the consumer; or

(D) intends to use the information in connection with a determination of the consumer's eligibility for a license or other benefit granted by a governmental instrumentality required by law to consider an applicant's financial responsibility or status; or

(E) otherwise has a legitimate business need for the information in connection with a business transaction involving the consumer.

Sec. 605. Obsolete information

(a) Except as authorized under subsection (b), no consumer reporting agency may make any consumer report containing any of the following items of information:

(1) Cases under Title 11 of the United States Code or under the Bankruptcy Act that, from the date of entry of the order for relief or the date of adjudication, as the case may be, antedate the report by more than 10 years.

(2) Suits and judgments which, from date of entry, antedate the report by more than seven years or until the governing statute of limitations has expired, whichever is

the longer period.

(3) Paid tax liens which, from date of payment, antedate the report by more than seven years.

(4) Accounts placed for collection or charged to profit and loss which antedate the report by more than seven years.

(5) Records of arrest, indictment, or conviction of crime which, from date of disposition, release, or parole, antedate the report by more than seven years.

(6) Any other adverse item of information which antedates the report by more than seven years.

(b) The provisions of subsection (a) are not applicable in the case of any consumer credit report to be used in connection with—

(1) a credit transaction involving, or which may reasonably be expected to involve, a principal amount of $50,000 or more;

(2) the underwriting of life insurance involving, or which may reasonably be expected to involve, a face amount of $50,000 or more; or

(3) the employment of any individual at an annual salary which equals, or which may reasonably be expected to equal, $20,000 or more.

Sec. 606. Disclosure of investigative consumer reports

(a) A person may not procure or cause to be prepared an investigative consumer report on any consumer unless—

(1) it is clearly and accurately disclosed to the consumer that an investigative consumer report including information as to his character, general reputation, personal characteristics, and mode of living, whichever are applicable, may be made, and such disclosure (A) is made in a writing mailed, or otherwise delivered, to the consumer, not later than three days after the date on which the report was first requested, and (B) includes a statement informing the consumer of his right to request the additional disclosures provided for under subsection (b) of this section; or

(2) the report is to be used for employment purposes for which the consumer has not specifically applied.

(b) Any person who procures or causes to be prepared an investigative consumer report on any consumer shall, upon written request made by the consumer within a reasonable period of time after the receipt by him of the disclosure required by subsection (a)(1), shall make a complete and accurate disclosure of the nature and scope of the investigation requested. This disclosure shall be made in a writing mailed, or otherwise delivered, to the consumer not later than five days after the date on which the request for such disclosure was received from the consumer or such report was first requested, whichever is the later.

(c) No person may be held liable for any violation of subsection (a) or (b) of this section if he shows by a preponderance of the evidence that at the time of the violation he maintained reasonable procedures to assure compliance with subsection (a) or (b).

Sec. 607. Compliance procedures

(a) Every consumer reporting agency shall maintain reasonable procedures designed to avoid violations of section 605 and to limit the furnishing of consumer reports to the purposes listed under section 604. These procedures shall require that prospective users of the information identify themselves, certify the purposes for which the information is sought, and certify that the information will be used for no other purpose. Every consumer reporting agency shall make a reasonable effort to verify the identity of a new prospective user and the uses certified by such prospective user prior to furnishing such user a consumer report. No consumer reporting agency may furnish a consumer report to any person if it has reasonable grounds for believing that the consumer report will not be used for a purpose listed in section 604.

(b) Whenever a consumer reporting agency prepares a consumer report it shall follow reasonable procedures to assure maximum possible accuracy of the

information concerning the individual about whom the report relates.

Sec. 608. Disclosures to governmental agencies

Notwithstanding the provisions of section 604, a consumer reporting agency may furnish identifying information respecting any consumer, limited to his name, address, former addresses, places of employment, or former places of employment, to a governmental agency.

Sec. 609. Disclosures to consumers

(a) Every consumer reporting agency shall, upon request and proper identification of any consumer, clearly and accurately disclose to the consumer:

(1) The nature and substance of all information (except medical information) in its files on the consumer at the time of the request.

(2) The sources of the information; except that the sources of information acquired solely for use in preparing an investigative consumer report and actually used for no other purpose need not be disclosed: Provided, that in the event an action is brought under this title, such sources shall be available to the plaintiff under appropriate discovery procedures in the court in which the action is brought.

(3) The recipients of any consumer report on the consumer which it has furnished—

> *(A) for employment purposes within the two-year period preceding the request, and*
> *(B) for any other purpose within the six-month period preceding the request.*

(b) The requirements of subsection (a) respecting the disclosure of sources of information and the recipients of consumer reports do not apply to information received or consumer reports furnished prior to the effective date of this title except to the extent that the matter involved is contained in the files of the consumer reporting agency on that date.

Sec. 610. Conditions of disclosure to consumers.

(a) A consumer reporting agency shall make the disclosures required under section 609 during normal business hours and on reasonable notice.

(b) The disclosures required under section 609 shall be made to the consumer—

(1) in person if he appears in person and furnishes proper identification; or

(2) by telephone if he has made a written request, with proper identification, for telephone disclosure and the toll charge, if any, for the telephone call is prepaid by or charged directly to the consumer.

(c) Any consumer reporting agency shall provide trained personnel to explain to the consumer any information furnished to him pursuant to section 609.

(d) The consumer shall be permitted to be accompanied by one other person of his choosing, who shall furnish reasonable identification. A consumer reporting agency may require the consumer to furnish a written statement granting permission to the consumer reporting agency to discuss the consumer's file in such person's presence.

(e) Except as provided in sections 616 and 617, no consumer may bring any action or proceeding in the nature of defamation, invasion of privacy, or negligence with respect to the reporting of information against any consumer reporting agency, any user of information, or any person who furnishes information to a consumer reporting agency, based on information disclosed pursuant to section 609, 610, or 615, except as to false information furnished with malice or willful intent to injure such consumer.

Sec. 611. Procedure in case of disputed accuracy

(a) If the completeness or accuracy of any item of information contained in his file is disputed by a consumer, and such dispute is directly conveyed to the consumer reporting agency by the consumer, the consumer reporting agency shall within a reasonable period of time reinvestigate and record the current status of that

information, unless it has reasonable grounds to believe that the dispute by the consumer is frivolous or irrelevant. If after such reinvestigation such information is found to be inaccurate or can no longer be verified, the consumer reporting agency shall promptly delete such information. The presence of contradictory information in the consumer's file does not in and of itself constitute reasonable grounds for believing the dispute is frivolous or irrelevant.

(b) If the reinvestigation does not resolve the dispute, the consumer may file a brief statement setting forth the nature of the dispute. The consumer reporting agency may limit such statements to not more than one hundred words if it provides the consumer with assistance in writing a clear summary of the dispute.

(c) Whenever a statement of a dispute is filed, unless there is reasonable grounds to believe that it is frivolous or irrelevant, the consumer reporting agency shall, in any subsequent consumer report containing the information in question, clearly note that it is disputed by the consumer and provide either the consumer's statement or a clear and accurate codification or summary thereof.

(d) Following any deletion of information which is found to be inaccurate or whose accuracy can no longer be verified or any notation as to disputed information, the consumer reporting agency shall, at the request of the consumer, furnish notification that the item has been deleted or the statement, codification, or summary pursuant to subsection (b) or (c) to any person specifically designated by the consumer who has within two years prior thereto received a consumer report for employment purposes, or within six months prior thereto received a consumer report for any other purpose, which contained the deleted or disputed information. The consumer reporting agency shall clearly and conspicuously disclose to the consumer his rights to make such a request. Such disclosure shall be made at or prior to the time the information is deleted or the consumer's statement regarding the disputed information is received.

Sec. 612. Charges for certain disclosures

A consumer reporting agency shall make all disclosures pursuant to section 609 and furnish all consumer reports pursuant to section 611(d) without charge to the consumer if, within thirty days after receipt by such consumer of a notification pursuant to section 615 or notification from a debt collection agency affiliated with such consumer reporting agency stating that the consumer's credit rating may be or has been adversely affected, the consumer makes a request under section 609 or 611(d). Otherwise, the consumer reporting agency may impose a reasonable charge on the consumer for making disclosure to such consumer pursuant to section 609, the charge for which shall be indicated to the consumer prior to making disclosure; and for furnishing notifications, statements, summaries, or codifications to person designated by the consumer pursuant to section 611(d), the charge for which shall be indicated to the consumer prior to furnishing such information and shall not exceed the charge that the consumer reporting agency would impose on each designated recipient for a consumer report except that no charge may be made for notifying such persons of the deletion of information which is found to be inaccurate or which can no longer be verified.

Sec. 613. Public record information for employment purposes

A consumer reporting agency which furnishes a consumer report for employment purposes and which for that purpose compiles and reports items of information on consumers which are matters of public record and are likely to have an adverse effect upon a consumer's ability to obtain employment shall—

(1) at the time such public record information is reported to the user of such consumer report, notify the consumer of the fact that public record information is being reported by the consumer reporting agency, together with the name and address of the person to whom such information is being reported; or

(2) maintain strict procedures designed to insure

that whenever public record information which is likely to have an adverse effect on a consumer's ability to obtain employment is reported it is complete and up to date. For purposes of this paragraph, items of public record relating to arrests, indictments, convictions, suits, tax liens, and outstanding judgments shall be considered up to date if the current public record status of the item at the time of the report is reported.

Sec. 614. Restrictions on investigative consumer reports

Whenever a consumer reporting agency prepares an investigative consumer report, no adverse information in the consumer report (other than information which is a matter of public record) may be included in a subsequent consumer report unless such adverse information has been verified in the process of making such subsequent consumer report, or the adverse information was received within the three-month period preceding the date the subsequent report is furnished.

Sec. 615. Requirements on users of consumer reports

(a) Whenever credit or insurance for personal, family, or household purposes, or employment involving a consumer is denied or the charge for such credit or insurance is increased either wholly or partly because of information contained in a consumer report from a consumer reporting agency, the user of the consumer report shall so advise the consumer against whom such adverse action has been taken and supply the name and address of the consumer reporting agency making the report.

(b) Whenever credit for personal, family, or household purposes involving a consumer is denied or the charge for such credit is increased either wholly or partly because of information obtained from a person other than a consumer reporting agency bearing upon the consumer's credit worthiness, credit standing, credit capacity, character, general reputation, personal characteristics, or mode of living, the user of such information shall, within a

reasonable period of time, upon the consumer's written request for the reasons for such adverse action received within sixty days after learning of such adverse action, disclose the nature of the information to the consumer. The user of such information shall clearly and accurately disclose to the consumer his right to make such written request at the time such adverse action is communicated to the consumer.

(c) No person shall be held liable for any violation of this section if he shows by a preponderance of the evidence that at the time of the alleged violation he maintained reasonable procedures to assure compliance with the provisions of subsections (a) and (b).

Sec. 616. Civil liability for willful noncompliance

Any consumer reporting agency or user of information which willfully fails to comply with any requirement imposed under this title with respect to any consumer is liable to that consumer in an amount equal to the sum of—

(1) any actual damages sustained by the consumer as a result of the failure;

(2) such amount of punitive damages as the court may allow; and

(3) in the case of any successful action to enforce any liability under this section, the costs of the action together with reasonable attorney's fees as determined by the court.

Sec. 617. Civil liability for negligent noncompliance

Any consumer reporting agency or user of information which is negligent in failing to comply with any requirement imposed under this title with respect to any consumer is liable to that consumer in an amount equal to the sum of—

(1) any actual damage sustained by the consumer as a result of the failure;

(2) in the case of any successful action to enforce any liability under this section, the cost of the action together with reasonable attorney's fees as determined by the court.

Sec. 618. Jurisdiction of courts; limitation of actions

An action to enforce any liability created under this title may be brought in any appropriate United States district court without regard to the amount in controversy, or in any other court of competent jurisdiction, within two years from the date on which the liability arises, except that where a defendant has materially and willfully misrepresented any information required under this title to be disclosed to an individual and the information so misrepresented is material to the establishment of the defendant's liability to that individual under this title the action may be brought at any time within two years after discovery by the individual of the misrepresentation.

Sec. 619. Obtaining information under false pretenses

Any person who knowingly and willfully obtains information on a consumer from a consumer reporting agency under false pretenses shall be fined not more than $5,000 or imprisoned not more than one year, or both.

Sec. 620. Unauthorized disclosures by officers or employees

Any officer or employee of a consumer reporting agency who knowingly and willfully provides information concerning an individual from the agency's files to a person not authorized to receive that information shall be fined not more than $5,000 or imprisoned not more than one year, or both.

Sec. 621. Administrative enforcement

(a) Compliance with the requirements imposed under this title shall be enforced under the Federal Trade Commission Act by the Federal Trade Commission with respect to consumer reporting agencies and all other persons subject thereto, except to the extent that enforcement of the requirements imposed under this title is *specifically committed to some other government agency under subsection (b) hereof. For the purpose of the exercise by the Federal Trade Commission of its functions and powers under the Federal Trade Commission Act, a violation of any requirement or prohibition imposed under this title shall constitute an unfair or deceptive act or practice in commerce in violation of section 5(a) of the Federal Trade Commission Act and shall be subject to enforcement by the Federal Trade Commission under section 5(b) thereof with respect to any consumer reporting agency or person subject to enforcement by the Federal Trade Commission pursuant to this subsection, irrespective of whether that person is engaged in commerce or meets any other jurisdictional tests in the Federal Trade Commission Act. The Federal Trade Commission shall have such procedural, investigative, and enforcement powers, including the power to issue procedural rules in enforcing compliance with the requirements imposed under this title and to require the filing of reports, the production of documents, and the appearance of witnesses as though the applicable terms and conditions of the Federal Trade Commission Act were part of this title. Any person violating any of the provisions of this title shall be subject to the penalties and entitled to the privileges and immunities provided in the Federal Trade Commission Act as though the applicable terms and provisions thereof were part of this title.*

(b) Compliance with the requirements imposed under this title with respect to consumer reporting agencies and persons who use consumer reports from such agencies shall be enforced under—

(1) section 8 of the Federal Deposit Insurance Act, in the case of:

(A) national banks, by the Comptroller of the Currency;

(B) member banks of the Federal Reserve System (other than national banks), by the Federal Reserve Board; and

(C) banks insured by the Federal Deposit Insurance Corporation (other than members of the

Federal Reserve System), by the Board of Directors of the Federal Deposit Insurance Corporation.

(2) section 5(d) of the Home Owners Loan Act of 1933, section 407 of the National Housing Act, and sections 6(i) and 17 of the Federal Home Loan Bank Act, by the Federal Home Loan Bank Board (acting directly or through the Federal Savings and Loan Insurance Corporation), in the case of any institution subject to any of those provisions;

(3) the Federal Credit Union Act, by the Administrator of the National Credit Union Administration with respect to any Federal credit union;

(4) the Acts to regulate commerce, by the Interstate Commerce Commission with respect to any common carrier subject to those Acts;

(5) the Federal Aviation Act of 1958, by the Civil Aeronautics Board with respect to any air carrier or foreign air carrier subject to the Act; and

(6) the Packers and Stockyards Act, 1921 (except as provided in section 406 of that Act), by the Secretary of Agriculture with respect to any activities subject to that Act.

(c) For the purpose of the exercise by any agency referred to in subsection (b) of its powers under any Act referred to in that subsection, a violation of any requirement imposed under this title shall be deemed to be a violation of a requirement imposed under that Act. In addition to its powers under any provision of law specifically referred to in subsection (b), each of the agencies referred to in that subsection may exercise, for the purpose of enforcing compliance with any requirement imposed under this title, any other authority conferred on it by law.

Sec. 622. Relation to State Laws

This title does not annul, alter, affect, or exempt any person subject to the provisions of this title from complying with the laws of any State with respect to the collection, distribution, or use of any information on consumers, except to the extent that those laws are inconsistent with any provision of this title, and then only to the extent of the inconsistency.

EFFECTIVE DATE

Sec. 602. Section 504 of the Consumer Credit Protection Act is amended by adding at the end thereof the following new subsection:

(d) Title VI takes effect upon the expiration of one hundred and eighty days following the date of its enactment.

And the Senate agrees to the same.

ABOUT THE AUTHOR

Bob Hammond is a free-lance writer and financial consultant. He is the author of *Credit Secrets: How to Erase Bad Credit* and has provided services to individuals, businesses, organizations, civic groups, and government agencies.